★ ★ ★
TICONDEROGA CRUISERS

BY CARLOS ALVAREZ

BELLWETHER MEDIA · MINNEAPOLIS, MN

Are you ready to take it to the extreme?
Torque books thrust you into the action-packed
world of sports, vehicles, and adventure. These books
may include dirt, smoke, fire, and dangerous stunts.
WARNING: read at your own risk.

Library of Congress Cataloging-in-Publication Data

Alvarez, Carlos, 1968-
 Ticonderoga cruisers / by Carlos Alvarez.
    p. cm. – (Torque: military machines)
 Summary: "Amazing photography accompanies engaging information about Ticonderoga cruisers. The
combination of high-interest subject matter and light text is intended for students in grades 3 through
7"–Provided by publisher.
 Includes bibliographical references and index.
 ISBN 978-1-60014-321-2 (hardcover : alk. paper)
 1. Cruisers (Warships)–United States–Juvenile literature. 2. Warships–United States–Juvenile
literature. I. Title.
 V820.3.A58 2010
 623.825'3–dc22
                                        2009037597

This edition first published in 2010 by Bellwether Media, Inc.

Printed in the United States of America, North Mankato, MN.
010110   1149

CONTENTS

THE TICONDEROGA CRUISER IN ACTION

A United States Navy **battle group** floats off the coast of an enemy nation. The enemy launches an air attack against the battle group. Dozens of fighter planes armed with **missiles** approach.

A Ticonderoga cruiser is ready to defend the battle group. The ship's **radar** tracks the enemy aircraft. Its weapons system helps the crew select targets and fire missiles. The enemy planes explode in the sky. The enemy's attack has failed. The Ticonderoga cruiser is too powerful.

Ticonderoga cruisers have four LM 2500 gas engines. They can reach speeds of more than 35 miles (56 kilometers) per hour.

GUIDED-MISSILE CRUISER

Cruisers are large, powerful combat ships. The Ticonderoga **class** is the only cruiser in the U.S. Navy.

Ticonderoga cruisers are armed with missiles, guns, **torpedoes**, and other weapons. Their **mission** is to protect other U.S. warships from enemy air attacks.

destroyer

cruiser

The Ticonderoga cruiser resembles a **destroyer** more than a classic cruiser. The U.S. Navy called it a cruiser because of its advanced missile system. The first Ticonderoga cruiser entered U.S. Navy service in 1981.

★ **FAST FACT** ★

Ticonderoga cruisers can carry two SH-60B Seahawk helicopters. The helicopters are used for transportation and search-and-rescue.

WEAPONS AND FEATURES

The Ticonderoga class is equipped with the **Aegis Combat System (ACS)**. This computer system links a ship's electronic sensors and weapons. The system helps the crew select targets and fire weapons. Advanced sensors help crews locate threats. The AN/SPY-1 radar system can track hundreds of targets at once. The AN/SQQ-89 **sonar** system searches for underwater threats.

Ticonderoga cruisers mainly use missiles to defend the fleet. Each ship carries MK41 vertical launch systems. Each MK41 has eight Tomahawk cruise missiles. These guided missiles lock on to a target. They can change direction while in flight. The cruisers may also carry SM-2 missiles to destroy airplanes.

MK41 vertical launch system

Only three other countries use cruisers in their navies.
They are Russia, France, and Peru.

Ticonderoga cruisers have other weapons to protect the fleet. Two MK 45 guns and two .50-caliber machine guns can fire at close targets. Torpedo launchers fire at surface ships and **submarines**. These weapons work with the missiles to attack all threats to the fleet.

.50-caliber machine gun

MK 45

TICONDEROGA CRUISER
SPECIFICATIONS:

Primary Function: Guided-missile cruiser

Length: 567 feet (173 meters)

Width: 252 feet (79 meters)

Displacement: 9,600 tons
        (8,700 metric tons)

Top Speed: 35 miles (56 kilometers)
        per hour

Engines: 4 General Electric LM 2500
        gas turbines

Crew: 364 (24 officers, 340 enlisted sailors)

TICONDEROGA CRUISER MISSIONS

The main mission of Ticonderoga cruisers is to protect other ships. They usually stay with a carrier battle group. These groups of warships are centered around huge **aircraft carriers**. Aircraft carriers are big, slow targets. They need combat warships to defend them.

Each Ticonderoga cruiser has a crew of 364. This includes officers and sailors. The captain is the officer in charge of the ship. Twenty-three officers help the captain carry out orders. The sailors perform the duties that keep the ship running. They also operate the sensor and weapons systems. Each crew member plays an important role in keeping cruisers ready for battle.

GLOSSARY

Aegis Combat System (ACS)—an advanced computer system that links a ship's sensors and weapons together

aircraft carrier—a huge Navy ship from which airplanes can take off and land; an aircraft carrier is like a floating airport.

battle group—warships that travel together to perform missions

class—a type or category

destroyers—small, fast warships that protect larger ships; destroyers are heavily armed.

missile—an explosive launched at targets on the ground or in the air

mission—a military task

radar—a sensor system that uses radio waves to locate objects in the air

sonar—a sensor system that uses sound waves to locate objects underwater

submarine—a warship that is able to travel underwater

torpedo—an explosive that travels underwater

TO LEARN MORE

AT THE LIBRARY

Alvarez, Carlos. *Arleigh Burke Destroyers*. Minneapolis, Minn.: Bellwether Media, 2010.

David, Jack. *The United States Navy*. Minneapolis, Minn.: Bellwether Media, 2008.

Zobel, Derek. *Nimitz Aircraft Carriers*. Minneapolis, Minn.: Bellwether Media, 2009.

ON THE WEB

Learning more about military machines is as easy as 1, 2, 3.

1. Go to www.factsurfer.com.

2. Enter "military machines" into the search box.

3. Click the "Surf" button and you will see a list of related Web sites.

With factsurfer.com, finding more information is just a click away.

INDEX